A Good Home

by Malcolm Higgins   illustrated by J. Conteh-Morgan

Harcourt

Orlando   Boston   Dallas   Chicago   San Diego

Visit *The Learning Site!*

www.harcourtschool.com

ISBN 0-15-325494-7

9 10 121 10 09 08 07 06 05 04

Ordering Options
ISBN 0-15-325468-8 (Collection)
ISBN 0-15-326572-8 (package of 5)

Pig did not like his home.
"Rabbit, you have a good home," he said. "I want a home like it."

"This is not a good home for you,"
said Rabbit. "It is too little."

"Crow, I like your home," he said.
"Can I have a home like it?"

4

"A nest is not a good home for you," said Crow. "It is up a tree."

"That is a nice home, Frog," Pig said. "I want a home like that."

"A pond is a bad home for you,"
said Frog. "You can not swim."

Pig went back to his pen.
"I like my home," he said.
"It is a very good home for me."